Is Faith
Irrational?

Booklets in the Searching Issues series:

Why Does God Allow Suffering?
What About Other Religions?
Is There a Conflict Between Science and Christianity?
What About the New Spirituality?
Does Religion Do More Harm Than Good?
Is the Trinity Unbiblical, Unbelievable and Irrelevant?
Is Faith Irrational?

Is Faith Irrational?

NICKY GUMBEL

Scripture quotations taken from the Holy Bible, New International Version Anglicised. Copyright © 1979, 1984, 2011 Biblica, formerly International Bible Society. Used by permission of Hodder & Stoughton Publishers, an Hachette UK company. All rights reserved. 'NIV' is a registered trademark of Biblica. UK trademark number 1448790.

Scripture quotations marked KJV are taken from The Authorized (King James) Version. Rights in the Authorized Version are vested in the Crown. Reproduced by permission of the Crown's patentee, Cambridge University Press.

Published by Alpha International
HTB Brompton Road
London SW7 1JA
Email: publications@alpha.org
Website: alpha.org@alphacourse

Illustrated by Charlie Mackesy

Contents

Is Faith
Irrational?

As a former atheist, I used to think that faith was completely irrational. It was only when I encountered Jesus Christ that it made sense to me. People often ask the question: is there any evidence for the Christian faith? Or, as some suggest, is faith irrational by its very definition? The philosopher Friedrich Nietzsche famously wrote that faith 'stands in opposition to all intellectual well-being'.

Christianity must have an answer, not only to particular searching issues, but also to the question of whether faith itself is baseless and irrational. This chapter will consider the question of whether it is irrational by considering five preliminary points about faith itself.

It takes faith to believe there is no God

It is exceedingly difficult, perhaps even impossible, to *disprove* God's existence. Most philosophers and scientists agree that you cannot conclusively disprove the existence of God, because it is almost impossible to prove a 'universal negative'. In fact, even many atheists would concede that it is impossible to prove that God does not exist.

In 2009, a coalition of British Atheists ran an advertising campaign with the slogan 'There *probably* is no God. Now stop worrying and enjoy your life' (italics mine). The word 'probably' was included in recognition of the fact that it is impossible to prove the non-existence of God. This in itself is a belief. Atheists *believe* that there is no God.

It is not only religious people who believe things: *everyone depends on certain beliefs.* Christians have beliefs. Atheists have beliefs. Even agnostics have beliefs. A friend once told me this story:

> Some time ago, during a slightly alcohol-assisted discussion on life, death and the origins of the universe, a friend turned to me and said, 'You're a man of faith, what do you think?'
>
> 'We are all men and women of faith,' I replied. 'Some of us have faith that there is a God, some of us have faith that there is no God, and neither position is provable.'
>
> 'Precisely,' he said, 'that's why I'm an agnostic.'
>
> 'You don't escape either,' I replied. 'You just have faith that it's not important to decide.'

Whether it is a question of God's existence, our worldview, or how we live, there is always an element of what we can call 'faith', whatever we *believe*. Not believing in God typically means believing in something else.

Faith is an essential part of knowledge

There is an element of belief or faith to every area of knowledge. Albert Einstein once said:

> The mechanics of discovery are neither logical nor intellectual. It's a sudden illumination, almost a rapture. Later, to be sure, intelligence and analysis and experiment confirm (or invalidate) the intuition. But initially there is a great leap of imagination.[1]

Legal decisions may also require a step of faith. I practised as a barrister for a number of years and am very aware that when a jury brings a guilty verdict it is a step of faith. They do not know that the defendant is guilty, rather they must trust the witnesses and the evidence given. Every verdict involves an element of faith.

Indeed, human relationships themselves, which are universal, are based on a kind of faith. In September 2007, Ms Yang, a 26-year-old daughter of a former bricklayer, became China's richest person and the wealthiest woman in Asia when her father passed on all his wealth to her. Her fortune amounted to $16.2 billion. Asked by a Hong Kong newspaper why he had handed over his fortune to his daughter, Mr Yang said, 'Even if I reach the age of 100, I am going to give it to her anyway. She is family and I have *faith* in her.'[2]

Faith is an important part of many aspects of life.

Faith and reason can be complementary

Faith involves belief and trust. Yet faith and reason do not by definition exclude each other; they can in fact be complementary. The Bible does not lead us towards a faith devoid of reason. Alongside the centrality of the heart and will, the New Testament also emphasises reason and the life of the mind.

Jesus said, 'Love the Lord your God with all your heart and with all your soul and with all your *mind*' (Matthew 22:37, italics mine). Jesus himself said, 'I am the truth' (John 14:6). Likewise, when Paul was on trial accused of being insane, he said, 'I am not insane... What I am saying is true and reasonable' (Acts 26:25). Paul affirmed a rational basis for his belief in Jesus, and he often spoke about his 'belief in the truth' (2 Thessalonians 2:13).

To be a Christian is to believe in the truth; there is rationality to faith. For this reason, the apostle Peter writes, 'Always be prepared to give an answer to everyone who asks you to give the reason for the hope that you have' (1 Peter 3:15).

Faith is rational, but faith also goes beyond reason in the context of relationship. Take as an example my relationship with my wife, Pippa. If asked whether my love for my wife was rational or irrational, I would say that it is not irrational at all. There are very good reasons for it; there is lots of evidence on which I base my love for her. Yet to say that my love for her is *merely* rational does not do justice to the relationship. A relationship involves more than just the mind: it involves the heart, the soul and every part of our being.

Love, like faith, is far greater and more all-encompassing than reason alone. In that sense, faith in God is rational, but also greater than reason itself. Pope John Paul II wrote:

Faith and reason... each without the other is impoverished and enfeebled... Deprived of reason, faith has stressed feeling and experience, and so runs the risk of no longer being a universal proposition. It is an illusion to think that faith, tied to weak reasoning, might be more penetrating; on the contrary, faith then runs the grave risk of withering into myth or superstition. By the same token, reason which is unrelated to an adult faith is not prompted to turn its gaze to the newness and radicality of being...

... Faith and reason are like two wings on which the human spirit rises in contemplation of the truth.[3]

Faith is never forced

Faith is like love. Love never coerces, and it is never forced. The knowledge of God is not forced upon people either, but is promised to those who seek him. Jesus said, 'Ask and it will be given to you; seek and you will find' (Matthew 7:7). The great French mathematical genius Blaise Pascal, who came to faith in Christ at the age of thirty-one, pointed out that God has provided enough evidence of himself to convince those of us who have open hearts and minds, but this evidence will never convince those who are closed to the idea of God:

> Willing to appear openly to those who seek Him with all their heart, and to be hidden from those who flee from him with all their heart, God so regulates the knowledge of Himself that He has given indications of Himself which are visible to those who seek Him and not to those who do not seek Him. There is enough light for those to see who only desire to see, and enough obscurity for those who have a contrary disposition.[4]

So the answer to the question, 'How much evidence is there?' is that there is not enough evidence to be coercive or to force belief, but there certainly is enough evidence to conclude that faith is by no means irrational. The writer of Hebrews defines faith by saying, 'Faith is... the *evidence* of things not seen' (italics mine, Hebrews 11:1, KJV).

Faith in Christ is also part of a relationship

For a Christian, faith is not simply about believing in something, but about trusting someone. Faith is like love. It is not only a matter of 'privately entertaining the opinion that a thing called "God" exists'.[5] Rather, faith is at the heart of a relationship – a relationship with a God who has made himself known in Jesus Christ. That is why the analogies that the New Testament writers use to describe this relationship are the terms used to describe the closest personal relationship: the relationship between a parent and a child, or a husband and a wife. This relationship of trust transforms our lives, as well as all our other relationships.

All relationships involve an element of trust – not only a relationship with God. Pope John Paul II said, 'There is no doubt that the capacity to entrust oneself and one's life to another person and the decision to do so are among the most significant and expressive human acts.'[6]

A relationship with God is indeed a matter of faith, but not at all a faith against all the evidence. What is this evidence that we base our faith on? Let us explore some of the reasons why faith is credible and viable in the modern world, by looking at the evidence of God the Creator, the evidence of Jesus and the evidence of transformed human lives.

Evidence of God the creator

The apostle Paul made the assertion that, 'Since the creation of the world God's invisible qualities – his eternal power and divine nature – have been clearly seen, being understood from what he has made' (Romans 1:20). He was clearly convinced of there being some sign or rumour of God in the creation itself. What is the evidence for this assertion?

Evidence from the fact that there is 'something rather than nothing'

As we look at the world around us, it is natural to wonder why it is here, or where it came from. Modern science has actually sharpened that question for us. 'The existence of the Big Bang begs the question of what came before that, and who or what was responsible.'[7] This view is often unpopular. As Stephen Hawking has written, 'Many people do not like the idea that time has a beginning, probably because it smacks of divine intervention.'[8] Einstein was among those who developed this view. He initially tried to resist the implication of his theory of General Relativity (that the universe has a beginning) by trying to formulate a model reconciling the theory with a static universe. He finally abandoned the attempt and accepted that the universe did have a beginning and the implication of 'the presence of a superior reasoning power', albeit while rejecting Judeo-Christian ideas of God.[9]

For many, this evidence points to the existence of God, but others (including Hawking himself) seek to provide alternative explanations. The question scientists attempt to answer is, 'If the Big Bang is how the world started, what caused the Big Bang?' Did it come from nothing? Or, is it possible to suggest it was caused by God?

In the final paragraph of his book, *God and the Astronomers*, the astrophysicist Robert Jawstrow wrote:

> At this moment it seems as though science will never be able to raise the curtain on the mystery of creation... Now we see how the astronomical evidence leads to a biblical view of the origin of the world. The details differ, but the essential

elements and the astronomical and biblical accounts of Genesis are the same; the chain of events leading to man commenced suddenly and sharply at a definite moment in time, in a flash of light and energy.[10]

Evidence from the 'fine tuning' of the universe

Although their answers differ, scientists such as Stephen Hawking have at least shown that, 'Even infinitesimally small differences in the original explosion that cosmologists see as the starting point of our universe would have resulted in a world where conscious life would not occur'.[11] If anything, the weight of the evidence for the fine-tuning of our universe and our world is on the increase.

Professor Anthony Flew was one of the most influential rationalist atheist philosophers. But in 2004, he changed his mind. The *Church Times* said, 'Flew... abandoned his life-long commitment to atheism and he now accepts that God exists. In his own words he "simply had to go where the evidence leads" and recognise that "the case for God is now much stronger than it was before".'[12]

Evidence of the nature of human beings

The philosopher David Hume pointed out that you cannot derive an 'ought' from an 'is'.[13] If things just are, as some atheists claim, then there cannot be absolute right and absolute wrong. But in that case, where does this innate sense of right and wrong that we all seem to carry within us – whether Christian, agnostic, or atheist – come from? Paul says that it is the way we are created. God made us with a conscience. He writes that the requirements of the law are written on our hearts. Sometimes they accuse and sometimes they defend us, because we have a conscience (Romans 2:15).

Another compelling piece of evidence to do with human nature is the longing that many find within themselves for something transcendent. St Augustine (AD 354–430) said, 'You formed us for yourself and our hearts are restless until they find their rest in you.'[14] This is the evidence of experience, the emptiness that is in every human heart. Deep down we know that material things alone cannot satisfy, and that even human relationships are not enough. Bernard Levin, perhaps the greatest columnist of his generation (and who was not a Christian), seemed to be only too aware of the inadequate answers to the meaning of life. He wrote:

> Countries like ours are full of people who have all the material comforts they desire, together with such non-material blessings as a happy family, and yet lead lives of quiet, and at times noisy, desperation, understanding nothing but the fact that there is a hole inside them and that however much food and drink they pour into it,

> however many motor cars and television sets
> they stuff it with, however many well balanced
> children and loyal friends they parade around
> the edges of it... it aches.[15]

This is human experience. Even in a secular society such as Britain, around 70 per cent of people claim to believe in God. How do we explain the fact that so many people in the world believe in God or are open to the possibility of God's existence? Many critics of religion suggest that people believe only because they were brought up that way. But, upbringing does not solve the question of why so many people believe.

A student once said to the great Archbishop of Canterbury William Temple, 'You believe what you believe because of the way you were brought up'. To which Temple replied, 'That is as may be. But the fact remains that you believe that "I believe what I believe because of the way I was brought up" because of the way you were brought up.'

Many have also suggested that religion is wish fulfilment. Yet, as C. S. Lewis pointed out, 'Such wish fulfilment would likely give rise to a very different kind of God than the one described in the Bible.'[16] The God of holiness and justice, who calls his followers to costly obedience and discipleship, teaching love and forgiveness, even of enemies, is certainly not the wished-for God of all and sundry!

Of course, wishing for something does not guarantee the existence or non-existence of that something. When St Augustine reflected on the God-shaped hole in every human heart, he was not suggesting that what is wished for must exist (though he certainly thinks it is a clue). Rather, St Augustine is pointing us to look at the peace, rest and joy that Christians testify to time and again in relationship with God.

Evidence of God the Liberator

People who profess Christian faith today can look not only to the evidence of creation and of human nature, but also to the historical life of Jesus Christ. John Stott has written:

> God is partly revealed in the ordered loveliness of the created universe. He is partly revealed in history and in experience, the human conscience, and the human consciousness... Nevertheless, God's full and final self-revelation... has been given in and through Jesus alone.... That is the reason why every enquiry into the truth of Christianity must begin with the historic Jesus.[17]

Evidence of the life of Jesus

No one seriously doubts the fact that there is a great deal of evidence for Jesus' existence. This comes not only from the Gospels and other Christian writings, but also from non-Christian sources. For example, the Roman historian Tacitus wrote that, 'Christ, from whom they [Christians] got their name, suffered the extreme penalty [ie, the crucifixion] during the reign of Tiberius at the hands of one of our procurators, Pontius Pilate.'[18]

There is plenty of evidence both inside and outside the New Testament for the existence of Jesus.[19]

Evidence for the death and resurrection of Jesus

Jesus Christ's physical resurrection from the dead is the cornerstone of Christianity. For myself, it was through the life, death and in particular the resurrection of Jesus that I came to believe that there is a God. Christians come to know who God is through these events of history into which God has entered. The world-renowned New Testament scholar Tom Wright said this:

> The Christian claim is not that Jesus is to be understood in terms of a God about whom we already know; it is this: the Resurrection of Jesus strongly suggests that the world has a Creator, and that that Creator is to be seen in terms of, through the lens of, Jesus.[20]

What is the evidence that the resurrection really happened? There are four historical facts in the Gospels that need to be examined:

- Jesus' burial
- The discovery of his empty tomb
- Eyewitness accounts of his post-mortem appearances
- The origin of the disciples' belief in his resurrection.

Tom Wright concludes his book *The Resurrection of the Son of God* by saying that we have to face two facts which, taken together, are extremely powerful:

> We are left with the secure historical conclusion: the tomb was empty, and various 'meetings' took place not only between Jesus and his followers... but also... between Jesus and people who had not been his followers. I regard this conclusion as coming in the same sort of category, of historical probability so high as to be virtually certain, as the death of Augustus in AD 14 or the fall of Jerusalem in AD 70.[21]

Wright also describes the explosion of Christianity that took place around the whole known world. He says, 'That is why as an historian, I cannot explain the rise of early Christianity unless Jesus rose again, leaving an empty tomb behind him.'[22]

Evidence of God the Transformer

For many people the most impressive evidence for the existence of God is the reality of transformed lives and transformed communities. The apostle Paul wrote, 'We... are being transformed into his likeness with ever-increasing glory, which comes from the Lord, who is the Spirit' (2 Corinthians 3:18).

Evidence of the transformed lives of Paul and the apostles

There is a great deal of historical evidence that the apostles' lives were transformed by what they believed to be an experience of the risen Jesus Christ and the outpouring of the Holy Spirit. Let us consider one example.

With astonishing suddenness, Paul, who had been persecuting the church, became the leading advocate of Christianity. What caused this turnaround? Paul was quite clear in his answer, 'Have I not seen Jesus our Lord?' (1 Corinthians 9:1). He lists the early appearances of Christ and then adds 'last of all he appeared to me also' (1 Corinthians 15:8). The book of Acts corroborates Paul's claim to have seen the risen Jesus (Acts 9:4 ff; Acts 22:7 ff; Acts 26:14 ff).

In the eighteenth century, two eminent lawyers, both atheists, Lord Lyttleton and Gilbert West, were absolutely determined to destroy the Christian faith. They made an agreement between them that they would do this by undermining two things: the resurrection of Jesus Christ and the conversion of St Paul.

In *Observations on the History and Evidences of the Resurrection of Jesus Christ*, Gilbert West set out to disprove Jesus' having risen from the dead. On the flyleaf of the book, West quoted Ecclesiasticus 11:7, 'Do not find fault before you investigate.' He sifted the evidence for the resurrection from a legal standpoint, and he finally become satisfied that Jesus was raised from the dead in the way the Gospels described.

Lord Lyttleton's book was entitled *Observations on the Conversion and Apostleship of St Paul*. He also studied the evidence from a legal standpoint, and he became convinced that Saul of Tarsus was converted in just the way described in Acts, becoming a radically new man. In the course of writing his book, Lyttleton too experienced a conversion and became a Christian. Of the evidence for the transformed life of St Paul, Lyttleton wrote, 'The conversion and apostleship of St Paul alone duly considered is in itself demonstration sufficient to prove Christianity to be a divine revelation.'[23]

Evidence of transformed lives and communities

The countless examples of transformed lives in church

history and of today offer further evidence of the rationality of faith. The conversion of St Augustine and the conversion of John Wesley number among them. Personally, I have heard innumerable stories of people whose lives have been transformed on Alpha at our church and around the world. A typical conversation might go:

> 'Were you a Christian?'
> 'No I wasn't.'
> 'What happened?'
> 'I encountered Jesus.'
> 'What difference has Jesus made to your life?'
> 'Well, he has transformed my relationship with my wife.'
> or 'Well, he's set me free from drug abuse.'
> or 'He's set me free from alcohol abuse.'

Francis Collins, former leader of the Human Genome Project, is one of today's leading scientists. Raised by freethinking parents, he became first an agnostic and then an atheist. He worked in medicine and recounts what happened:

> I was raised by... freethinking parents... for whom religion was just not very important.... I became first an agnostic and then an atheist... One afternoon, a kindly grandmother with only

a few weeks to live shared her own faith in Jesus quite openly with me, and then asked, 'Doctor, what do you believe?'... I fled the room, having the disturbing sense that the atheist ice under my feet was cracking, though I wasn't quite sure why. And then suddenly the reason for my disquiet hit me: I was a scientist. I was supposed to make decisions based on evidence. And yet I had never really considered the evidence for and against faith. As I explored the evidence more deeply, all around me I began to see signposts to something outside of nature that could only be called God. I realized that the scientific methods can really only answer questions about HOW things work. It can't answer questions about WHY – and those are in fact the most important ones. Why is there something instead of nothing? Why does mathematics work so beautifully to describe nature? Why is the universe so precisely tuned to make life possible? Why do we humans have a universal sense of right and wrong and an urge to do right... Confronted with these revelations, I realized that my own assumption – that faith was the opposite of reason – was incorrect. I should have known better: Scripture defines faith as 'the substance of things hoped for, the evidence of things not seen'. Evidence! Simultaneously,

I realized that atheism was in fact the least rational of all choices... How could I have had the arrogance to make such an assertion? After searching for two years more, I ultimately found my own answer – in the loving person of Jesus Christ. Here was a man unlike any other. He was humble and kindhearted. He reached out to those considered lowest in society. He made astounding statements about loving your enemies. And he promised something that no ordinary man should be able to promise – to forgive sins. On top of all that having assumed all my life that Jesus was just a myth, I was astounded to learn that the evidence for his historical existence was actually overwhelming. Eventually, I concluded the evidence demanded a verdict. In my 28th year, I could no longer deny my need for forgiveness and new life – and I gave in and became a follower of Jesus. He is now the rock upon which I stand, the source for me of ultimate love, peace, joy, and hope.[24]

Time after time after time, all around the world, millions of people are experiencing the risen Christ today. This is evidence. It is not just individual lives that have been transformed, but whole communities.

The church itself is evidence. The church has made a difference to the lives of billions of men and women.

It has had an impact on society, on culture, on the arts, and on philosophy. It has had an impact on family life, on the dignity of human beings, on the rights of children, on care for the poor, for the sick, for the dying and the homeless.

Evidence of transformed understanding

C. S. Lewis said, 'I believe in Christianity as I believe that the Sun has risen, not only because I see it, but because by it I see everything else.'[25] Not only can you can see the rising sun, but by it you see everything else that is around you. Lewis's point was that coming to faith gives a whole new understanding of this world.

St Anselm of Canterbury said, '*Credo ut intelligam*' (I believe in order that I might understand). This is very similar to the way that science works. First, you come up with a theory, and then you test it with the evidence. It is through belief that we come to understand the world – belief in Jesus, '… in whom are hidden all the treasures of wisdom and knowledge' (Colossians 2:3). Our understanding of the purpose of this universe comes through faith.

Faith is certainly not irrational. In fact, its relationship with reason is an ongoing process. In Pope John Paul II's book *Fides et Ratio* (*Faith and Reason*), following a chapter entitled '*Credo ut Intelligam* (I believe in order that I might understand) there is a chapter entitled '*Intelligo ut Credo*' (I understand in order that I might believe). In other words, when you come to believe, you don't stop exploring.

Today's prevailing cultural attitude is to assume that Christians just stop thinking. This is simply not the case: when you become a Christian you become, if anything, *more* interested in everything. You start exploring God's universe. Reason, in the context of relationship, is given permission to question, to investigate and to go on learning.

Two examples of how Christianity transforms our understanding of the world are the twin stories of creation and the fall. The doctrine of creation gives a context to the ubiquity of beauty – that there is something noble about every human being.

The doctrine of the fall explains why nothing is ever quite perfect – both in the created world and also in the human heart. Aleksandr Solzhenitsyn, the great Russian novelist, wrote, 'The line separating good and evil passes not through states, nor between classes, nor between political parties either, but right through every human heart, and through all human hearts.'[26]

This is the understanding that the Bible gives us in order to make sense of the world. Faith can make sense of religion, atheism, the human mind, the rational structure of the universe, justice and friendship. Most of all, faith makes sense of love.

Perhaps love is the most powerful transfiguration of human understanding. If this world has no God, if it just came about, how do we explain love? British theologian Graham Tomlin writes of how the reality of love offers us two possibilities:

> At the end of the day there is a simple choice to be made. Is love a 'misfiring instinct', an accidental by-product of evolution, and a thinly veiled strategy for personal or genetic survival? Or is it actually the centre of reality, the reason why we are here? For Christians, it is the very centre of all that we are. We are made in the image of a God who is love and we were made to learn to love and to be loved. That is the whole meaning of our existence. Christians suggest that we have a deep instinct that tells us that love is no accidental by-product, a 'blessed mistake' but is in fact the very centre of the human experience of human life and happiness.[27]

Conclusion

I can only conclude with my own experience. I started out life as an atheist. When I was a teenager I argued against Christianity for a long time. I started to investigate further when two very good friends, Nicky and Sila Lee, told me that they had become Christian. I was concerned for them and this gave me an incentive to look into it.

I started to read the New Testament. I didn't read the Gospels as the inspired word of God; I simply read them as historical documents. Yet, to me they had a ring of truth. I saw that there was evidence for Jesus and I had to make a choice. It certainly was not wish fulfilment because at that moment my thinking was that, if Christianity was true and if I was to become a Christian, life was going to be terrible! However, I thought that, if it was true, I had to become a Christian. So I said 'yes', thinking that really was the end of all enjoyment of life.

The moment I made that step, I experienced the living Jesus Christ, the risen Jesus Christ, and I realised that this was what I had actually been searching for all my life without knowing it. I wasn't conscious of a God-shaped gap, but I was always searching for the next thing with which to try to satisfy it.

When I experienced that relationship with God through Jesus Christ, my longing was satisfied. I experienced God's love for me through the Holy Spirit. It broke my belief that everything we do in life is selfish. I began to realise that, if there is a God, he can break through with his love and give us a freedom to love that makes such a difference to our lives. This is what I have experienced in the last forty years.

Life has not always been easy since then. There is the dark night of the soul, there are painful experiences of doubt and suffering, all kinds of things that challenge our faith, and more. But my experience has been that there really is good evidence for our faith. Our faith is not irrational; it is rational. It is also beyond rationality – it is relationship, relationship with the God who made us. For me, the key thing is to be able to say, along with the apostle Paul and along with countless others, 'I know whom I have believed' (2 Timothy 1:12).

Endnotes

1. The conversation is reported in John Dominic Crossan, *The Dark Interval: Towards a Theology of Story* (Argus Communications, 1975), p.31.
2. *The Times*, 9 October 2007, p.55.
3. John Paul II, *Fides et Ratio –Encyclical Letter of Pope John Paul II* (Catholic Truth Society, 1998), p.3.
4. Blaise Pascal, *The Pensées: Thoughts, Letters and Minor Works*, Section VII, 430.
5. Quoted in Lash, 'Where Does The God Delusion Come From?', *New Blackfriars Magazine*, p.512.
6. John Paul II, *op cit*, p.50.
7. Francis Collins, *The Language of God* (Simon & Schuster, 2007) p.66.
8. Stephen Hawking *A Brief History of Time From the Big Bang to Black Holes* (Bantam Press, 1988) p.46.
9. Hugh Ross, *The Fingerprint of God* (Promise Publications, 1991), page number unknown.
10 Robert Jawstrow, *God and the Astronomers* (W. W. Norton, 1992), pp.107,14.
11. Stephen Hawking *A Brief History of Time From the Big Bang to Black Holes* (Bantam Press, 1988), p.46.
12. Paul Badman, *Church Times* , 26 October 2007.
13. David Hume, 1738, reference unknown.
14. St Augustine, *Confessions*, Book 1, Section 1.
15. By kind permission of Bernard Levin.
16. Francis Collins, *op cit*, p.37.
17. John Stott, *Authentic Christianity*, (Inter-Varsity Press, 1996), p.47.
18. The Roman historian Tacitus, concerning the 'Great Fire of Rome' in *Annals*, Book 15, Chapter 44 (c. 116).
19. For a more in-depth discussion on the historical evidence for Jesus' existence please see 'Who is Jesus?' and 'Why Did Jesus

Die?' in Nicky Gumbel, *Questions of Life* (Alpha International, 2010).

20. N. T. Wright, *The Resurrection of the Son of God* (Fortress Press, 2003), p.170.

21. *Ibid.*

22. N. T. Wright, 'The New Unimproved Jesus,' *Christianity Today*, 13 September 1993.

23. Lord Lyttleton, *Observations of the Conversion and Apostleship of St. Paul* (1747).

24. Remarks delivered by Francis S. Collins at the 55th Annual Prayer Breakfast, 1 February 2007 in Washington DC, USA.

25. C. S. Lewis, *The Weight of Glory: And Other Addresses* (HarperOne, 2001), p.116.

26. Aleksandr Solzhenitsyn, *The Gulag Archipelago 1918–1956* (1973).

27. Graham Tomlin, 'Dawkins – A Theologian's Perspective' in Nicky Gumbel, *Is God a Delusion?* (Alpha International, 2008), p.108

Further Reading

Richard Bauckham, *Jesus and the Eyewitnesses*
(William B. Eerdmans, 2008)

William Lane Craig, *Reasonable Faith* (Crossway, 2008)

Tim Keller, *The Reason for God* (Hodder & Stoughton, 2009)

Amy Orr-Ewing, *But is it Real?* (IVP, 2008)
and *Why Trust the Bible?* (IVP, 2008)

Alpha

Alpha is a practical introduction to the Christian faith, initiated by HTB in London and now being run by thousands of churches, of many denominations, throughout the world. If you are interested in finding out more about the Christian faith and would like details of your nearest Alpha, please visit our website:

alpha.org

or contact:
The Alpha Office,
HTB Brompton Road,
London,
SW7 1JA

Tel: 0845 644 7544

About the Author

Nicky Gumbel is the pioneer of Alpha. He read law at Cambridge and theology at Oxford, practised as a barrister and is now vicar of HTB in London. He is the author of many bestselling books about the Christian faith, including *Questions of Life*, *The Jesus Lifestyle*, *Why Jesus?*, *A Life Worth Living*, *Searching Issues* and *30 Days*.